VIZCAYA
MUSEUM & GARDENS

VISIONS OF

VIZCAYA

© Vizcaya Museum and Gardens, 2006

DIRECTOR'S FOREWORD

The view from Vizcaya's *parterres*, or decorative hedges, looking toward the Secret Garden.

International Harvester Vice President James Deering (1859–1925) built Vizcaya, his winter home, between 1914 and 1922. Now known as Vizcaya Museum and Gardens, the extraordinary estate is an accredited museum and National Historic Landmark belonging to the citizens of Miami-Dade County. Our mission is to preserve Vizcaya to engage our community and its visitors in learning through the arts, history, and the environment.

Many visitors wonder about the meaning of the name "Vizcaya," and there are several theories about its origin. The estate's name—like Biscayne Bay, on which it sits—hearkens back to the northern Spanish province known as Vizcaya, or Biskaia, suggesting the project's significant European inspiration. In a 1915 letter, Deering stated his desire to perpetuate "the myth" that Vizcaya was named after an explorer,[1] further imbuing the project with associations of foreign discovery and exchange.

Guests of Vizcaya are invited to enjoy Deering's Mediterranean-inspired main house and formal gardens, which are picturesquely sited between the sparkling waters of Biscayne Bay and a lush hardwood forest, or hammock. These same natural elements were pivotal in the Chicago businessman's selection of the site nearly one hundred years ago. The main house is distinguished for its architecture and its lavishly designed interiors, filled with European, Asian, and American artifacts spanning two millennia.

Unlike many other house museums from this era, Vizcaya still possesses almost all of its original furnishings, offering an experience of great historic integrity. The gardens are notable for introducing a European design aesthetic to a subtropical context—a daring premise that resulted in early and ongoing experiments to identify appropriate plant specimens. While Vizcaya's style evokes faraway places, local stone, soil, and plants reflect Deering's desire to showcase Miami and its natural beauty.

Originally, the 180-acre estate included a lagoon dotted with manmade islands, to the south of Vizcaya's manicured gardens, and a village, on the west side of South Miami Avenue, with fields for grazing livestock and growing produce. Deering built the village with the intent of making Vizcaya virtually self-suffi-cient. This idea evoked the spirit of European precedents while compensating for the limited services and commodities available in early twentieth-century Miami. The village's buildings housed staff quarters, an automobile garage, workshops, and an array of barns for domesticated animals. Fortunately, the village survives, and its splendid collection of buildings is in the process of being restored for public enjoyment.

Vizcaya is a powerful lens through which to consider creators and consumers of the arts. It likewise informs our understanding of the relationships among leisure and industry, history and innovation, and nature and design. As a Miami project built by a leading American in a European aesthetic, Vizcaya also provides insight into the local, national, and international contexts that have shaped our world, past and present. This book offers a brief introduction to the people and ideas behind Deering's remarkable undertaking.

Thanks to Vizcaya Deputy Director for Collections and Curatorial Affairs, Dr. J. Laurie Ossman, who authored the informative text and managed the production of this book. Since her arrival in 2004, Dr. Ossman has contributed keen intellect and insight to the interpretation of Vizcaya. We are grateful to photographer Bill Sumner for his spectacular color images, created specifically for this publication.

Mr. Sumner's enthusiasm for Vizcaya is apparent in his generous and eye-opening photographs, which capture the rich and subtle values of the estate. Thanks also to Peter Roman, principal of Inkbyte Design, who is responsible for the handsome layout of this publication, which suits its subject well. We appreciate the efforts of Lea Nickless Verrecchia, who coordinated this project, and of Vizcaya Marketing Director Holly Blount, who assisted with production. Additional gratitude to historian and Founding Vizcaya Museum and Gardens Trust Chair Arva Moore Parks, volunteer Lynn M. Summers, Vizcaya Collections and Archives Manager Remko Jansonius, and editor Leslie Sternlieb for their contributions to the publication.

Vizcaya is a destination for visitors from around the world and a vital community resource. The reasons to preserve and celebrate this special place are clear and numerous. Although the care of this aging and fragile property is daunting, we have many partners in this pursuit. In 2004, Miami-Dade voters approved an unprecedented bond initiative that will greatly facilitate its restoration. Moreover, we benefit from the ongoing support of the Vizcaya Museum and Gardens Trust, The Vizcayans, the Vizcaya Volunteer Guides, and the Miami-Dade County Board of County Commissioners, Mayor, County Manager, Department of Cultural Affairs, and Cultural Affairs Council. We hope this memento of Vizcaya enhances your knowledge, rouses your imagination, and triggers your interest to learn more.

DR. JOEL M. HOFFMAN
JANUARY 2006
EXECUTIVE DIRECTOR
VIZCAYA MUSEUM AND GARDENS

---

1 Letter, James Deering to Paul Chalfin, 6 July 1915, box "Metals," folder "Silver," Vizcaya Museum and Gardens Archives. There was, in fact, a Spanish merchant by the name of Sebastián Vizcaíno, who explored the coast of California in 1602.

JAMES DEERING: VIZCAYA'S PATRON

In February 1913, fifty-three-year-old James Deering sat in his father's house in Coconut Grove, Florida, with designer Paul Chalfin and architect F. Burrall Hoffman, Jr., poring over floor plans for a house on Biscayne Bay. The magnificent Mediterranean-inspired villa depicted on the draftsman's paper—a house, formal gardens, and a village—was far more elaborate than what the younger Deering had originally intended. Yet, the ambitious plan to create such a complex and sophisticated place in the middle of the subtropical wilderness fired his imagination. No private residence of this scale had been attempted in Florida before. The technological and human challenge of creating a highly ordered and complex series of settings for the display and enjoyment of rare and fragile artworks, both indoors and out, seemed exceptionally daunting—if not impossible. The journey that led from a sketch on a dining room table to the establishment of Miami's cultural jewel, one of the most celebrated estates in America, is the story of Vizcaya.

James Deering was born in South Paris, Maine, the son of William Deering and his second wife, Clara Hammond Deering. William Deering, who had inherited a family wool mill, invested in land in the western United States and financially backed the development of agricultural machinery to make his property more valuable. In 1873, he moved his family to Illinois and assumed control of a farm equipment manufacturer, renaming it the Deering Harvester Company. Deering Harvester enabled farmers to harvest an acre of grain in an hour—a dramatic increase in productivity that allowed commercial agriculture in the West to be more profitable. As more reapers were sold, Deering's land investments grew in value, and, by the end of the nineteenth century, the Deerings became one of America's wealthiest families.

James Deering's older half-brother, Charles, graduated from the United States Naval Academy and studied art in Paris before entering the family business. James attended Northwestern University and the Massachusetts Institute of Technology before joining the Deering Harvester Company in 1880.

By the turn of the century, James Deering owned homes on Lakeshore Drive in Chicago and in nearby Evanston, as well as in New York City and at Neuilly-sur-Seine, near Paris. Deering appeared in social columns as an active partygoer, traveler, and cultural ambassador, hosting visiting French dignitaries at his homes in New York and Chicago. For his work in promoting agricultural technology in France, James Deering was appointed to the Legion of Honor in 1906.

In 1902, in a deal brokered by banker John Pierpont Morgan, the Deering Harvester Company merged with the McCormick Reaper Company and others to form International Harvester, the largest producer of agricultural machinery in the nation. James Deering became vice president of the firm, charged with oversight of the Illinois manufacturing plants. As William Deering's health weakened, the family began spending winters in St. Augustine, Florida, and then, by 1910, William Deering purchased land and built a home in Coconut Grove, just south of Miami. In 1910, James began to plan his own home in Miami.

View of Casino Mound Cascade, c. 1953.

Left
William Deering,
who first brought
his sons James and
Charles to visit
the Miami area
around 1903.
This photograph
probably dates
from the 1880s.

Above (left to right)
J. Summer,
Charles Deering,
James Deering,
and S. W. Baylis,
c. 1915. Summer
and Baylis were
the valets of the
Deering brothers.

Mouth of the Miami River, Miami, Fla.

Above, left
Brickell Point,
Miami, 1905.
The Deering broth-
ers rented houses in
this area before
they built their own
homes. Courtesy
Florida State Library
and Archives.

Above, right
James Deering
(second from left),
W. J. Matheson
(right), and friends,
c. 1913. Matheson,
a successful pigment
and chemical
manufacturer,
was the leading
developer of the
Coconut Grove
area of Miami.

Right
Charles Deering's
estate, south
of Miami,
photographed
by renowned
botanist John
Kunkel Small, 1916.
Courtesy Florida
State Library
and Archives.

A Passion for the Past

The Marine Garden at Vizcaya, featuring stone peacocks designed by eminent French sculptor Gaston Lachaise, c. 1953.

By the turn of the century, James Deering's world was one in which travel, art collecting, and building great estates were the favored extracurricular activities of America's corporate and social elite. In the decades following the Civil War, the rise of industry created unparalleled wealth and technological achievement in America. As a result, artists and patrons alike sought a visual language for expressing the nation's cultural ascendancy. Because many of the greatest artistic achievements of the Italian Renaissance were sponsored by merchant families, such as the Medici and Strozzi, leaders of America's new industrial society—families like the Vanderbilts, Harrimans, Rockefellers, and Morgans—saw themselves as the appropriate heirs to this classically inspired tradition. The 1893 World's Columbian Exposition in Chicago, commemorating the four-hundredth anniversary of Christopher Columbus's voyage to the New World, used classical architecture to assert the nation's claim to cultural leadership. Not content to equal the past, American builders and arts patrons sought to surpass it by embracing modern methods and materials, reinventing the built landscape with steel frames and mechanized equipment. These new structures became a metaphor for the country's claim to having established a new "American Renaissance" in architecture and the arts.

As aristocratic fortunes in Europe declined, American collectors saw the opportunity to import the best of the European cultural tradition, in the form of art and design, to the United States, where they would eventually become part of museums and related public collections. Like others of their acquaintance—Berthe Honoré Palmer, Isabella Stewart Gardner, and J. P. Morgan—James Deering and his half-brother, Charles, both collected European art. In addition to purchasing important paintings by Francisco Goya, El Greco, and Francisco de Zurbarán, Charles maintained lifelong friendships with contemporary painters John Singer Sargent, Anders Zorn, and Gari Melchers. James Deering owned important works by Edouard Manet and Giovanni Battista Tiepolo, which he bequeathed to the Art Institute of Chicago.

Patrons of the American Renaissance also traveled extensively in Europe, where they acquired a taste for architectural styles and decorative arts of the past. They hired American architects to produce modern versions of their favorite *palacio, château,* or *villa* for their city houses and country estates.

With designer Paul Chalfin's guidance, Deering assembled a diverse collection at Vizcaya that represented many cultures and periods of art—as wide-ranging as ancient Roman sculpture, Renaissance tapestries, Chinese ceramics, Rococo and Neoclassical furniture, and even modern art from his own time. The objects were intended to initiate erudite conversation as well as admiration. Chalfin's eye for world-class antiques enhanced Vizcaya's physical beauty with an air of connoisseurship. For example, they gathered the Banquet Hall's fifteenth-century Flemish *mille-fleurs* tapestry, the Renaissance Hall's Hispano-Moresque "Admiral" carpet, and the Fountain Garden's ancient Roman altar. Like many prominent collectors in the American Renaissance, Deering especially prized artifacts associated with famous historical personages. These pieces served as conversation-starters as well as relics of the heroic past. At Vizcaya, the Banquet Hall's pair of Ferrara tapestries that had once graced poet Robert Browning's Venetian palazzo might spark a discussion of poetry while the Breakfast Room's Ming ceramics and Chinoiserie might prompt talk of the political unrest in China following the recent abdication of the "last emperor," in 1912. Beds associated with Emma, Lady Hamilton (the infamous mistress of British naval hero Admiral Lord Nelson), and Napoleon's sister, Pauline Borghese (whose partially nude reclining pose was rendered by Antonio Canova in his sculpture *Venus Victrix*), may have inspired more risqué storytelling. Vizcaya's eclectic collection also incorporated contemporary art, showcasing sculpture by Gaston Lachaise, A. Stirling Calder, Duilio Cambellotti, and Charles Cary Rumsey, as well as paintings by Robert W. Chanler and Paul Thévenaz in gardens and outdoor spaces. James Deering's architects and designers conceived of Vizcaya as a centuries-old villa, or Italian country estate, as a framework to unite these select treasures from ancient times to the present. While grand, august estates like Vizcaya struck some observers as "conspicuous consumption," their creators viewed them as living models of good design that would provide a cultural legacy for future generations.

Seventeenth-century Italian limestone statue depicting the myth of Leda and the Swan.

Far left
Elsie de Wolfe
(right; pictured here
with companion
Elisabeth Marbury)
pioneered the estab-
lishment of interior
design as a profes-
sion. She suggested
that James Deering
consult her advisor
Paul Chalfin on the
purchase of antiques
for Vizcaya.

Left, top
Chicago socialite
and patron of the
arts Berthe Honoré
Palmer, a longstand-
ing friend of James
Deering, encour-
aged his interest in
formal garden
design. Courtesy
Library of Congress.

Left, bottom
Isabella Stewart
Gardner's Venetian-
style house in
Boston, 1904. Paul
Chalfin and James
Deering knew Mrs.
Gardner and her
house, and Vizcaya
undoubtedly shares
the spirit of her
collection's highly
personal mix of
Renaissance treasures,
theatrical settings,

and works by
contemporary artists
in their circle.
Courtesy Library
of Congress.

Above
James Deering's
house at Neuilly-
sur-Seine, just
outside Paris, c. 1910.

Biltmore, in Asheville, North Carolina, was the epitome of the American Renaissance country estate, including a grand house, formal gardens, adjacent woodland, and village for support services and staff, c. 1900. Courtesy Library of Congress.

Villa La Pietra, near Florence, Italy. In the summer of 1914, Deering and Chalfin stayed here as guests of Sir Arthur Acton, who introduced them to Diego Suarez, his landscape architect. Suarez drew on La Pietra and other nearby villas while designing the formal gardens at Vizcaya. Courtesy Villa La Pietra, New York University, Florence.

THE VISION
PAUL CHALFIN

Vizcaya's chief designer, Paul Chalfin (1874–1959), grew up in a prosperous family in Midtown Manhattan. As a child, Chalfin frequently visited his grandfather's art-filled townhouse, located just across the street from the legendary Italian Renaissance-style home of railroad magnate William H. Vanderbilt. After two years at Harvard University, Chalfin left to pursue a painting vocation at New York's Art Students League, followed by three years of study at the prestigious École des Beaux-Arts in Paris. The École des Beaux-Arts trained painters, sculptors, and architects in the techniques, forms, and symbols of the classical tradition, as handed down from antiquity through the Renaissance to modern times. The American artists and architects who studied there became the leaders of the so-called American Renaissance, mastering old traditions and invigorating them to serve the new society of the Industrial Age. After working for three years as curator of Asiatic arts at the Museum of Fine Arts in Boston, Chalfin returned to Europe in early 1906 for a painting fellowship at the American Academy in Rome. He studied and traveled in Italy for two more years, returning to New York in 1909. Although exquisitely trained as a painter in the classical tradition and highly refined in personal manner, Chalfin remained mostly unemployed.

PAUL CHALFIN

Because of Chalfin's European education and reputation for sophisticated taste, socialite and interior decorator Elsie de Wolfe hired him as an advisor on antiques and decorative arts. One of their first projects together was the redecoration of some rooms in the Chicago home of James Deering. Three years later, when Deering approached de Wolfe about designing the interiors for a house he was planning to build in Miami, she declined. Thinking Miami too distant and rustic to hold any interest for her, she recommended Paul Chalfin in her stead. Chalfin ignited Deering's imagination, while also, more practically, acting as his land agent, negotiating the purchase of several tracts from local landowner Mary Brickell. According to Chalfin, Brickell drove a hard bargain, arguing, "Two hundred feet of waterfront is enough for any man, even Jimmy Deering."[2] Deering ultimately acquired 180 acres for Vizcaya's house, gardens, and village, at the same time preserving the surrounding native hardwood forest.

Perhaps realizing that he was never going to succeed as a painter, Paul Chalfin invested his considerable knowledge of art, design, and history into the creation of Vizcaya. He devised an elaborate series of rooms radiating from the courtyard of the house, linking visually to garden spaces that led to paths, streams, and bridges, and increasingly less formal landscapes that ultimately faded into the adjacent woodland. James Deering initially envisioned a substantial but unpretentious Spanish-style house in a rustic hammock setting. Deering's vision became the canvas on which Paul Chalfin imagined and, ultimately, created Vizcaya—the American Renaissance ideal of a country estate.

[2] Paul Chalfin, interview by Robert Tyler Davis, transcript, May 1956, Robert Tyler Davis papers, Smithsonian Institution Archives, RU 7439, box 4, folder 20.

THE ARCHITECTURE
F. BURRALL HOFFMAN, JR.

F. Burrall Hoffman, Jr.,
c. 1910. Courtesy
private collection.

Vizcaya's architect, F. Burrall Hoffman, Jr. (1882–1980), was born into a wealthy New York City family. In 1896, his father hired the architecture firm of Carrère and Hastings to build a townhouse for his family on East Seventy-ninth Street. Enthralled with the design and construction processes, the teenaged Hoffman decided to become an architect. He studied at Harvard University and subsequently attended the École des Beaux-Arts in Paris, then the preeminent architectural training program in the world. Hoffman returned to the United States in 1905 and began his career as a draftsman in the office of Carrère and Hastings. He worked on prestigious country residences such as E. H. Harriman's Arden House in upstate New York and Alfred I. duPont's Nemours estate in Delaware. Around 1910 Hoffman became acquainted with Paul Chalfin, when the designer asked him if he would lecture at the Colony Club, a newly founded women's social organization in New York City. Later that year, Hoffman left Carrère and Hastings to establish his own architectural practice. In 1912, Chalfin again approached Hoffman. This time he asked if Hoffman would be interested in designing a house "for an art collector." The architect accepted,

F. BURRALL HOFFMAN, JR.

and soon discovered that the collector in question was James Deering, and the "house" would become Vizcaya.

The Beaux-Arts design process customarily began with the development of the building plan, and ended with ornamentation and furnishings. But, at Vizcaya, Hoffman reversed the process and created a spatial framework for the decorative elements and artworks that Chalfin and Deering had already collected. Hoffman was up to the design challenge, but soon found himself caught between the two, as the designer and client debated everything from the shape of the north garden stairs to the placement of specific statues. Eventually, after Hoffman designed most of the buildings for the Vizcaya village, Chalfin's insistence on controlling the entire design process drove him from the project. Phineas Paist, best known today for his architectural achievements in the planned city of Coral Gables, oversaw the completion of the village. Hoffman went on to enjoy a long and successful career as a residential architect for affluent clients in Manhattan and Palm Beach. Hoffman's challenge at Vizcaya had been to create buildings that fulfilled the ideal collector's environment, at least as Deering—and, more particularly, Chalfin—envisioned it.

THE GARDENS
DIEGO SUAREZ

Diego Suarez at Vizcaya, 1967.

Vizcaya's landscape designer, Diego Suarez (1888–1974), was born in Bogotá, Colombia, the great-grandson of Venezuelan revolutionary leader Francisco de Miranda. Following the death of Suarez's father in 1906, the family moved to Florence, Italy, where Diego studied architecture at the Accademia di Belle Arti (the Italian equivalent of the French École des Beaux-Arts). Graduating in 1912, he established a garden design practice and grew interested in reviving formal Italian Renaissance gardens, which had been supplanted in many places by the more informal, naturalistic eighteenth- and nineteenth-century English style. Suarez became acquainted with Sir Arthur Acton, whose American wife had recently purchased the fifteenth-century Villa La Pietra in the foothills outside Florence. The two determined to restore the villa's gardens as illustrations of proper gardening principles.

DIEGO SUAREZ

In June 1914, Acton asked Suarez to show two American guests—James Deering and Paul Chalfin—the best formal gardens of the region, many of which were illustrated in American novelist Edith Wharton's popular nonfiction book *Italian Villas and Their Gardens*. Suarez later noted that Chalfin "took photographs of EVERYTHING he saw: fountains, vistas, statues, urns, etc.," collecting images to incorporate into the design of Vizcaya.[3] A few months later, Suarez traveled to New York and found himself stranded there after the outbreak of the First World War. By chance, he again encountered Chalfin, who offered him work designing the gardens for James Deering's Miami estate. Initially, Suarez based his designs on those of the sixteenth-century Villa Lante, near Viterbo, the epitome of Italian formal garden design by Giacomo Barozzi da Vignola. But when he visited Miami for the first time, Suarez realized that the Italian design would not work at the Florida site. Most notably, the main garden axis from the Tea Room to the south, where a lake stood, was not the ideal Renaissance expression of divine geometry and perspective, but rather revealed a blinding reflection of the subtropical sunshine from the adjacent lake. Suarez cleverly adapted his design and created the Mound as the new focal point of the gardens, thus shielding the house from the harsh reflections, and lending drama to the vista from the small structure known as the Casino. Suarez created exaggerated perspective lines using low hedges, or *parterres*, fanning out from the South Terrace, to dramatize the formal geometry of the gardens. He also incorporated motifs from various sites he had shown Chalfin and Deering on their visit to Italy.

Following a series of disagreements with Chalfin, Suarez left the project in 1917, and, for many years, Chalfin took credit for the garden design. Suarez later married Chicago heiress and philanthropist Evelyn Marshall Field, and pursued landscape architecture as well as diplomatic missions on behalf of Colombian-American relations. Even in later life, Suarez could recite the models for various gardens and elements at Vizcaya—just as the gardens themselves were to conjure the best examples from Italian history and carry forward the classical tradition into the unique South Florida landscape.

3 Diego Suarez, interviewed by Kathryn Chapman Harwood, transcript, c. 1956, box "Personnel," folder "Suarez," Vizcaya Museum and Gardens Archives.

Photograph of a design model of Vizcaya made by Menconi Brothers, New York, 1914. Certain elements of the completed building, such as the eaves in the center section, changed during construction.

Far left
Surveying instruments
in the hammock
pathway that would
become the main
formal approach
to Vizcaya, 1913.

Left
Site of Deering's
future house facing
Biscayne Bay, with
the first trench
for construction,
late 1913.

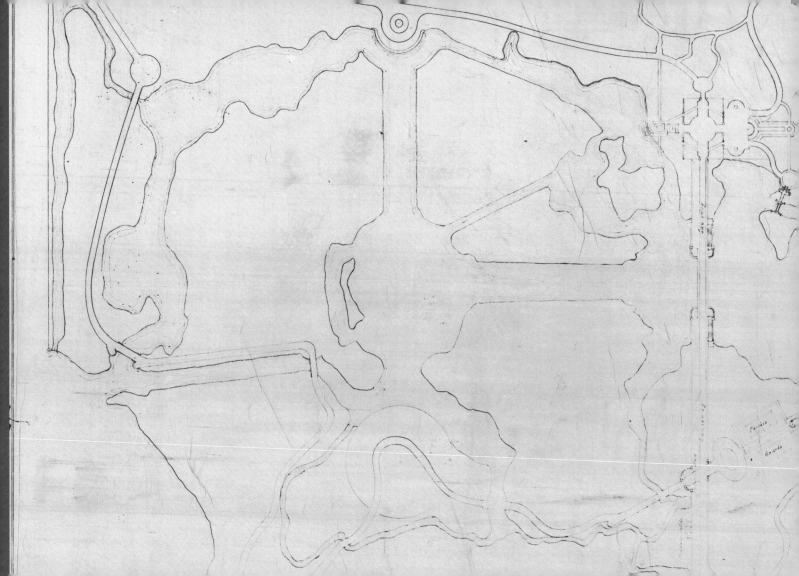

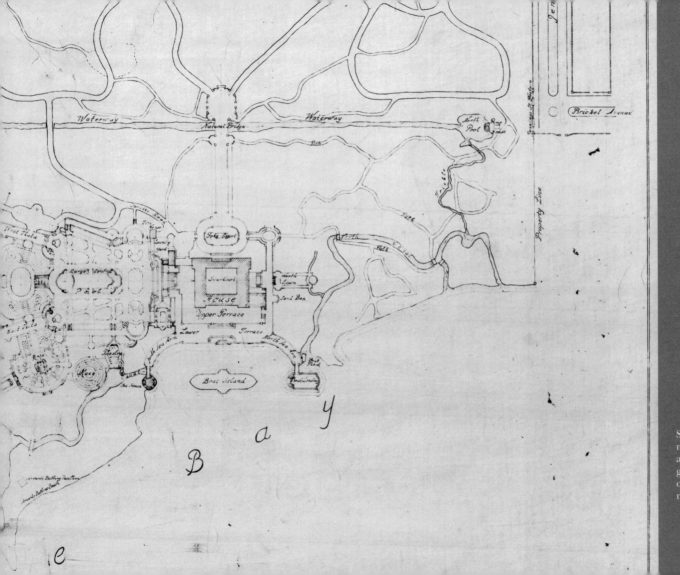

Site plan of the
main house
and formal
gardens, ink
on linen, 1916,
revised 1922.

THE CONSTRUCTION OF VIZCAYA

View of South
Terrace and
gardens, under
construction, from
the incomplete
Tea Room,
December 1915.

The first excavations for Vizcaya began in 1912, when the population of Miami was little more than ten thousand. By 1920, more than one thousand of the town's citizens had been employed on some aspect of Vizcaya's house, gardens, and village, demonstrating the estate's impact on the community.

Paul Chalfin assembled a team of internationally known artists and Italian, German, Scottish, Irish, and Czech craftsmen (by way of New York), along with Bahamian stonemasons, from nearby Coconut Grove. He combined their skills with those of local builders, familiar with the climate and its challenges, to create a unified vision from a diverse range of traditions. Photographers took weekly construction photographs and sent them to James Deering to keep him current on the project. These images vividly illustrate the harsh, dense, natural environment the builders faced, and the enormity of the task of creating a Mediterranean-style villa in the midst of a subtropical wilderness. In 1914, with the shell of the main house nearly complete, Chalfin wrote to his friend Sir Arthur Acton: "It is almost as imposing as the Palazzo Pitti," he said. "If you can imagine the Palazzo Pitti standing on a lagoon in Africa."[4]

THE CONSTRUCTION OF VIZCAYA

J. B. Orr, whose company played a pivotal role in the construction of Vizcaya, recalled that Deering visited the site every day when he was in Miami, and always stopped to talk with the workers. Vizcaya's workers, in turn, called the millionaire art collector and patron "Mr. Jimmy." Orr also recollected that Chalfin, who was known in New York as a social butterfly and snob, "talked the language of the workmen" and "took a personal interest in their work." The designer's diplomatic skills were surely put to the test when he insisted early in construction that workers building the first masonry walls along Thirty-second Avenue cast aside their modern equipment and continue the job using "only those tools available to early Italians."[5]

Although Paul Chalfin tended to downplay the patron's role in the creative process, correspondence clearly shows that James Deering was actively involved in all aspects of Vizcaya's design and construction, from the selection of technological gadgetry (such as the central vacuum-cleaning system, fire alarms, and state-of-the-art electric refrigerator) to the placement of sculpture on the grounds. Deering's comments also reflected his desire to make Vizcaya comfortable as a home. His concern with livability often challenged the designers' preferences for establishing purely artistic effects. For example, Deering instructed Hoffman to block the open vista from the main house's Entrance Loggia, through the open courtyard to the bay, in order to give himself a bit of privacy.

But Deering's correspondence with Chalfin was always cordial, if occasionally animated by a hint of impatience, with the willful designer. Deering disagreed with Chalfin's choice of gold and blue for the awnings and gondola poles, because he felt they competed with the tones of the water and sunshine, while Chalfin felt they echoed them. In this case, Chalfin prevailed. Deering, however, overruled Chalfin most of the time, as when he insisted on the placement of the statues in the "piazza" at the top of the driveway, so "that both 'Vizcaya' and 'Ponce de Leon' are seen on the journey from the entrance gate to the house."[6] This level of involvement—requiring the prominent location of statues of mythical and historical explorers—indicates that Deering came to see Vizcaya not only as a home, but also as a metaphorical tribute to the spirit of adventure in Florida's past and present.

4 Letter, Paul Chalfin to Sir Arthur Acton, partial transcript, 23 February 1915, box "Personnel," folder "Acton," Vizcaya Museum and Gardens Archives.

5 J. B. Orr, interviewed by Robert Tyler Davis, notes, 17 February 1954, Robert Tyler Davis papers, Smithsonian Institution Archives, RU7439, box 4, folder 20.

6 Letter, James Deering to Paul Chalfin, 17 April 1919, box "Stone," folder "Sculpture," Vizcaya Museum and Gardens Archives. See page 3 on Deering's desire to communicate the idea that Vizcaya was named after an explorer.

Left, top
George Sykes, superintendent of construction at Vizcaya, 8 June 1914.

Left, bottom
Vizcaya's first construction office, located where the main entrance gate to the estate now stands, 1914.

Above, left
Foundation trench for the northeast corner of the main house, 1914. For practical reasons, Chalfin wanted to site the main house at a higher elevation, but Deering wanted it as close to the bay as possible.

Above, right
Construction equipment where the main formal gardens now stand, May 1915. Visible are the trestle for transporting supplies (left), the concrete mixer (center), and the water tower (right).

Far left
Vizcaya's steel framing and rein-forced concrete, seen here in the fall of 1914, were state-of-the-art tech-nology for the era.

Left
Masons carving stone inside the unfinished Banquet Hall, 1915.

Opposite
Main house under
construction,
6 May 1915.

Right, top
Sixteenth-century
French mantel in
the Renaissance
Hall, before the
addition of an upper
section designed by
Paul Chalfin, 1916.

Right, bottom
James Deering's
Sitting Room,
during the installa-
tion of decorative
millwork, 1916.

Far right, top
View from the
courtyard to the
front door, before
the vista was
blocked by the
installation of the
Bacchus Fountain
in the Entrance
Loggia, 1916.

Far right, bottom
Stonecutter turning
a column of
local limestone
on site, 1915.

Construction view
toward the main
house, from the
entrance to the
Rose Garden, 1916.

Rose Garden just
after the installation
of the fountain, but
prior to plantings,
summer 1916.

Left, top
The Barge before the installation of A. Stirling Calder's monumental figural sculptures, 1915.

Left, bottom
A worker posing with one of Vizcaya's European statues, which were uncrated in the village before being transported by cart to the formal gardens for placement, 1916.

Above
Stonecutters install a sixteenth-century French garden arch in the Secret Garden, 1916. These local craftsmen then carved native stone elements to blend the antique piece seamlessly into the new setting.

Left
The village Garage housed James Deering's Packard motorcars, such as the one seen in the archway.

Above
The shadehouse in the Vizcaya village allowed gardeners to grow vegetables and flowers for the estate in all seasons.

Opposite
The Vizcaya village, 1917.

A Visit to the House

The entry drive to Vizcaya's main house.

Left to right: The Entrance Loggia; detail of bronze doors in the Entrance Loggia.

The Entrance Hall.

Left to right: The Reception Room; James Deering's Library.

James Deering's Library.

Left to right: Door in the North Hallway; view toward the courtyard from the North Hallway.

Left to right: The Telephone Room; detail of statue in the Renaissance Hall; an Italian altarpiece conceals pipes in the Renaissance Hall's Welte-Mignon pipe organ.

Left to right: Renaissance Hall; model caravel in the East Loggia.

The East Loggia.

The Barge.

Left to right: Bust of a faun (a mythological woodland spirit); detail of a door in the East Loggia; nineteenth-century Italian tall case clock in the north arcade.

Detail of a console depicting river gods in the Music Room.

The Music Room.

The Banquet Hall.

The Tea Room ceiling.

The Tea Room.

Stained glass doors in the Tea Room.

Left to right: The Butler's Pantry; detail of a call box for staff (top); a plate from Deering's formal service of 24-karat gold-rimmed Royal Crown Derby china, ordered through Tiffany & Co. (bottom).

Left to right: Giltwood wall bracket in the form of a "mer-man" in the South Arcade; the South Arcade; the main staircase.

The Cathay Bedroom.

Left to right: The original elevator cab used by James Deering and his guests; detail of a nineteenth-century Italian giltwood *torchière* (lamp stand), and an eighteenth-century English mailbox, both in the second-floor gallery.

James Deering's private Sitting Room.

James Deering's Bedroom.

Left to right: James Deering's Bath; a guest sitting room, named "Galleon."

The Breakfast Room.

The Kitchen.

THE GARDENS AND BEYOND

Statues dating from ancient Rome to the eighteenth century line Vizcaya's garden walkways.

The south façade of the main house, as seen from the gardens.

The gardens, as seen from the South Terrace of the main house.

The Casino (meaning "little house" in Italian).

The Casino ceiling, featuring a center panel by Swiss painter Paul Thévenaz.

Two parlors in the Casino offered James Deering's guests an elegant retreat within the gardens.

View of the main house from the top of the Casino Mound.

The Fountain Garden, named for the sixteenth-century Italian fountain at its center, as seen from the Casino Mound.

Left to right: A terra-cotta statue of Flora, the goddess of flowers, in the main gardens; the West Vista at the base of the Casino Mound.

The Maze Garden.

Orchids have long been featured at Vizcaya and were originally displayed in the Secret Garden.

The David A. Klein Orchidarium, where orchids are displayed today.

The West Gate Lodge, where Mr. Deering's chauffeur lived, marks the entrance to the Vizcaya village.

The Garage was the first Vizcaya village building to be restored.

The estate's waterfront includes a lattice Tea House.

Sunrise over Biscayne Bay, from the main house; the seahorse, seen here atop the weathervane, is a recurring motif at Vizcaya.

LIFE AT VIZCAYA

Vizcaya's east façade.

James Deering first witnessed Vizcaya's completed main house on Christmas Day, 1916. According to accounts of the occasion, Chalfin staged an elaborate theatrical ceremony for Deering's arrival by Venetian gondola: miniature antique cannons fired a salute, and friends dressed in Chalfin-designed Italian peasant costumes danced to Italian folk music. Chinese lanterns hung from trees in the gardens, illuminating the immature plantings and gravel paths that stood as signs of still greater things to come. Construction of the gardens—ultimately encompassing an artificial lake and several islands that no longer exist—continued until 1922.

Maintaining the house and gardens of Vizcaya proved almost as great an undertaking as building it. Although James Deering initially planned to spend only about four months each winter at Vizcaya, a large staff was required to maintain the estate throughout the year. Between sixteen and eighteen staff members maintained the house, and at least twenty-six gardeners and workers remained to safeguard the estate and keep the formal gardens impeccable during Deering's absence.

When James Deering was in residence, he hosted elaborate parties, often at lunchtime, for visiting luminaries such as film stars Lillian Gish and Marion Davies, politician and orator William Jennings Bryan, inventor Thomas Edison, and President Warren G. Harding, as well as family and less famous friends. Deering presented Hollywood films to entertain his guests; he especially favored the films of Charlie Chaplin. Several silent films used Vizcaya as a location, however it is said that when Deering saw Russian actress Alla Nazimova's rearrangement of the Pantaloon guest room to serve as her dressing room, he declared that no more movies would be made at Vizcaya. Deering reputedly swam in the pool only once (and did not extinguish his cigarette while doing so). But he encouraged friends and family to swim, as well as their children, who made castles in the nearby sandbox and played hide-and-seek in the gardens.

To help Deering maintain the illusion of carefree luxury, housekeeper Cecilia Adair and twelve of her staff members were readily available, and lived in rooms on the mezzanine and third floor of Vizcaya's two western towers. Deering insisted that one male staff member reside in the main house, as a security measure. Other household staff lived in the village or in homes nearby, and walked or rode bicycles to work each day. In spite of innovations such as the central vacuum system, running Vizcaya to Deering's standards was a monumental task. Laundry was done by hand and dried in discreetly walled yards. Carpets, curtains, and linens were removed, cleaned, and stored at the end of the season. Each summer, every book in the library was wrapped in newspaper to discourage insect infestation. It required constant vigilance to combat the mold and mildew naturally encouraged by the humid subtropical climate, especially since Vizcaya's courtyard was originally open to the sky and weather. Deering owned pet monkeys and birds, which also required care in his absence. In addition, a chauffeur, a French chef, a pastry chef, and the estate superintendent lived at the Vizcaya village.

The village, located across what is now South Miami Avenue, was built between 1917 and 1922 to house staff and support life in the main house. A greenhouse supplied fresh flowers, fruit, and vegetables for Deering, his guests, and staff. A herd of cows provided milk, and chickens furnished a ready supply of fresh eggs. A farm stand sold surplus eggs and produce, although the income generated was surely negligible. On the precious bayfront property, Deering and Chalfin set aside an area for staff members to use as their own private beach. A simple dance platform encouraged recreation after a day's hard work. Although Deering was a perfectionist, domestic employee Eustace Edgecombe later recalled that, upon visiting the staff dining room, he personally removed a sign with guidelines for behavior, as he "didn't wish to impose on them in their own quarters."[7] Fearful of the destructive force of fire, Deering had three fire wagons and a tank wagon housed on the estate, just behind the main house. To arrest any blazes before they became catastrophic, water connections were scattered throughout the hammock, as well as near the buildings.

After years of suffering from pernicious anemia, today a treatable disease, in 1925 James Deering died onboard an ocean liner returning to the United States from France. Many staffers stayed on at Vizcaya after his death to care for the estate and ensure its well-being. During the ten years Deering spent at Vizcaya, no major hurricane tested the strength of his ideal estate. The year after his death, however, the first of several major hurricanes devastated the gardens and challenged the resilience of Vizcaya and the people who remained to care for it.

James Deering maintained two yachts at Vizcaya: *Psyche* (top) and *Nepenthe* (bottom).

7 Interview, Eustace Edgecombe, notes, no date, box "Personnel," folder "Edgecombe," Vizcaya Museum and Gardens Archives.

VIZCAYA BECOMES A PUBLIC MUSEUM

Children enjoying
a sphinx in
the gardens.

Following James Deering's death, his half-brother Charles's daughters, Barbara Deering Danielson and Marion Deering McCormick, acquired full ownership of Vizcaya and its surrounding lands. In 1934, the family contacted Paul Chalfin to take steps toward opening the estate as a museum. He arranged for new plantings for the gardens (where some non-native plants had failed to thrive) and oversaw some minor rearrangement of furniture as well as repairs to damaged outdoor statuary and structures. They opened Vizcaya as a museum, but after operating for only a brief period in 1935 a major hurricane again devastated the estate, making the task of maintaining Vizcaya even more overwhelming. In the 1940s, the family sold the southern gardens and grounds to the Archdiocese of Miami, while they negotiated an agreement to turn over Vizcaya to Dade (now Miami-Dade) County as an art museum. In 1952, the heirs sold the main house, village, and grounds to Dade County for $1 million, and donated all the collections and furnishings to the county. In support of the new institution, volunteers organized the Vizcaya Volunteer Guides in 1954 to conduct tours of the house. In 1956, civic-minded individuals also formed The Vizcayans to develop community involvement and private funding for the museum.

Maintaining Deering's collection of fragile artwork, furnishings, and elaborate gardening schemes has proven an ongoing challenge for Vizcaya's museum professionals, as it was for Deering's own staff. In its original configuration, Vizcaya's open courtyard left rooms open to the outdoors, with the full environmental impact of subtropical weather, salt air, harsh sunlight, and pests. To help preserve the house and its collections, the courtyard was enclosed and air conditioning installed in 1986. In August 1992, Hurricane Andrew caused severe damage to the gardens, and storm surge waters flooded the basement, reaching the level of the first floor. Fortunately, and partly thanks to the courtyard roof, the house was spared from catastrophic loss, although restoration and repair continued for nearly a decade. Subsequent hurricanes have again tested Vizcaya.

In 1998, the Miami-Dade Board of County Commissioners designated the Vizcaya Museum and Gardens Trust as the governing body for Vizcaya. In 2004, Miami-Dade County voters approved the Building Better Communities bond program, funding from which underwrites major restoration and enhancements for the main house, gardens, and village.

Throughout its history as a public museum, Vizcaya has attracted millions of local residents and visitors from across the globe to enjoy the site, participate in events and programs, and commemorate special moments in their lives. Vizcaya is a magnet for amateur and commercial photographers, and several major Hollywood films have featured the estate. Over the years, Vizcaya has also served as a diplomatic seat for Miami-Dade County, having hosted major international events such as the gathering of thirty-four heads of state attending the first Summit of the Americas in 1994. Among the numerous dignitaries who have visited the estate are Queen Elizabeth II, Pope John Paul II, Presidents Ronald Reagan and Bill Clinton, and King Juan Carlos I and Queen Sofia of Spain.

Because of continuous, rigorous preservation efforts, this pioneering estate is available for the general public to enjoy today. Visitors to Vizcaya learn about the arts, history, and the environment, and, ultimately, how they interrelate in the world. Vizcaya's visitor experience will become increasingly dynamic through the rehabilitation and interpretation of additional historic facilities in the coming years.

Vizcaya's subtropical setting means that the estate has been subject to severe damage from hurricanes and tropical storms. Among the most severe have been (top to bottom) an unnamed tropical storm (1966); Hurricane Andrew (1992); and Hurricane Wilma (2005).

Vizcaya is a favorite location for elegant special events and photo shoots (including those for young women celebrating their *quinceañera*, or fifteenth birthday).

Visitors of all ages are invited to enjoy educational programs at Vizcaya.

Ongoing conservation of historic artifacts ensures the preservation of Vizcaya and its collections for future generations.

Damaged peacock statues (designed by Gaston Lachaise) being removed from the Marine Garden for conservation treatment, 2005.